D1307967

MYSTERIES OF SCIENCE

NEAR–DEATH EXPERIENCES

THE UNSOLVED MYSTERY

BY LISA WADE McCORMICK

Reading Consultant:
Barbara J. Fox
Reading Specialist
North Carolina State University

Content Consultant:
Jody A. Long
Near-Death Experience Research Foundation
www.nderf.org

Capstone
press

Mankato, Minnesota

Blazers is published by Capstone Press,
151 Good Counsel Drive, P.O. Box 669, Mankato, Minnesota 56002.
www.capstonepress.com

Library of Congress Cataloging-in-Publication Data
McCormick, Lisa Wade, 1961–
   Near-death experiences: the unsolved mystery/by Lisa Wade McCormick.
   p. cm. — (Blazers. Mysteries of science)
   Includes bibliographical references and index.
   Summary: "Presents the mystery of near-death experiences, including descriptions, theories,
and famous examples" — Provided by publisher.
   ISBN-13: 978-1-4296-2329-2 (hardcover)
   ISBN-10: 1-4296-2329-2 (hardcover)
   1. Near-death experiences — Juvenile literature. I. Title.
BF1045.N4M38 2009
133.901'3 — dc22   2008028696

Editorial Credits
Lori Shores, editor; Alison Thiele, designer; Marcie Spence, photo researcher

Photo Credits
Alamy/Blackout Concepts, 26–27; Carol and Mike Werner, 14–15; Classic Image, 22–23;
   Paul Kuroda, 20–21; Peter Casolino, 18–19
AP Images/Lefteris Pitarakis, 8–9
Corbis/C. Lyttle/zefa, 10–11
Fortean Picture Library, 12–13
Getty Images Inc./Henrik Sorensen, 6–7
Landov LLC/Klaus Rose/dpa, 24–25
Shutterstock/Lane V. Erickson, cover; lucwa, 28–29; Marilyn Volan, grunge background
   (throughout); Maugli, 16–17 (background); Nick Alexander, 4–5; rgbspace, (paper art
   element) 3, 17; Shmeliova Natalia, 16 (paper art element)

1 2 3 4 5 6 14 13 12 11 10 09

TABLE OF CONTENTS

A DOCTOR DIED, OR DID HE?

A car ran over Dr. George Rodonaia in 1976. Rescue workers said he died instantly. They left his body in a **morgue** for three days.

morgue — a place where dead bodies are kept

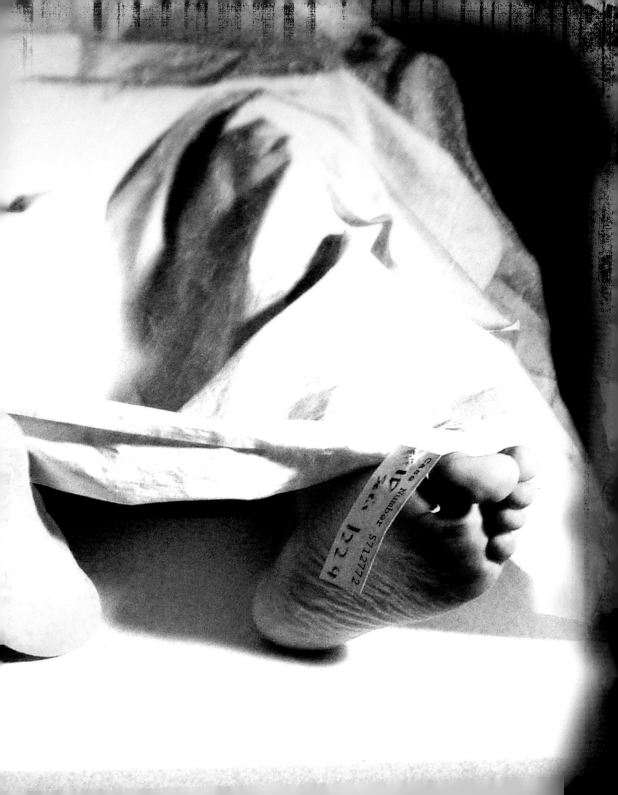

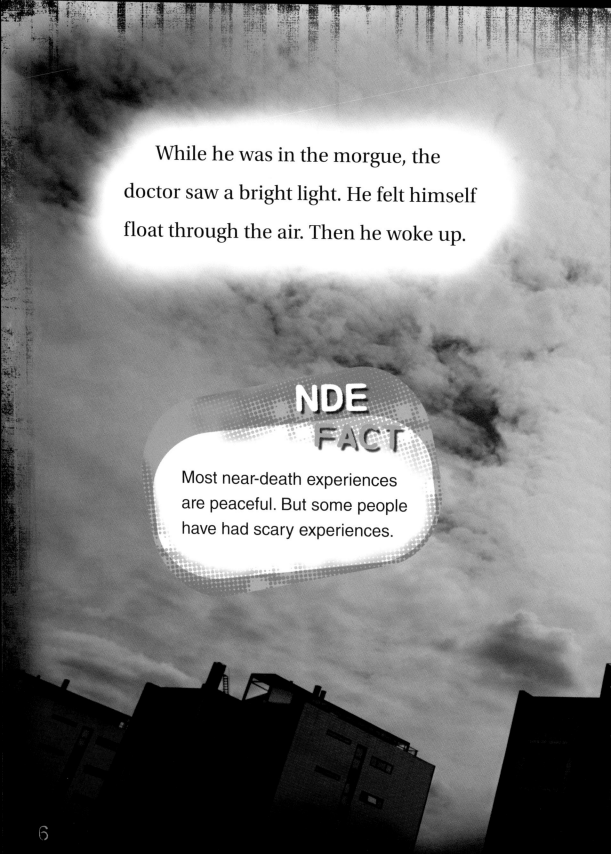

While he was in the morgue, the doctor saw a bright light. He felt himself float through the air. Then he woke up.

NDE FACT

Most near-death experiences are peaceful. But some people have had scary experiences.

What happened to George Rodonaia? Did he have a strange dream? Or was it a near-death experience (NDE)?

NDE
FACT

During most NDEs, a person
either stops breathing or has
no pulse for five to 15 minutes.

AMAZING EXPERIENCES

An NDE happens when a person dies but is **revived**. Stories about these strange events are told around the world.

revive — to bring someone back to life

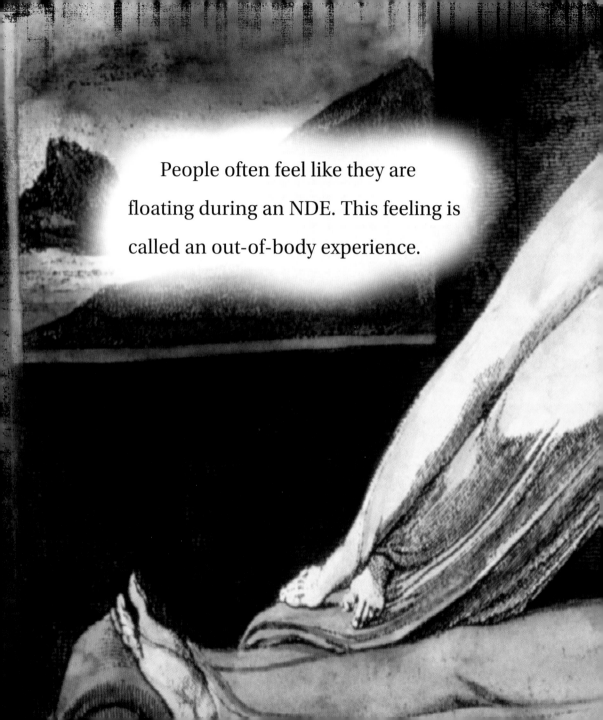

People often feel like they are floating during an NDE. This feeling is called an out-of-body experience.

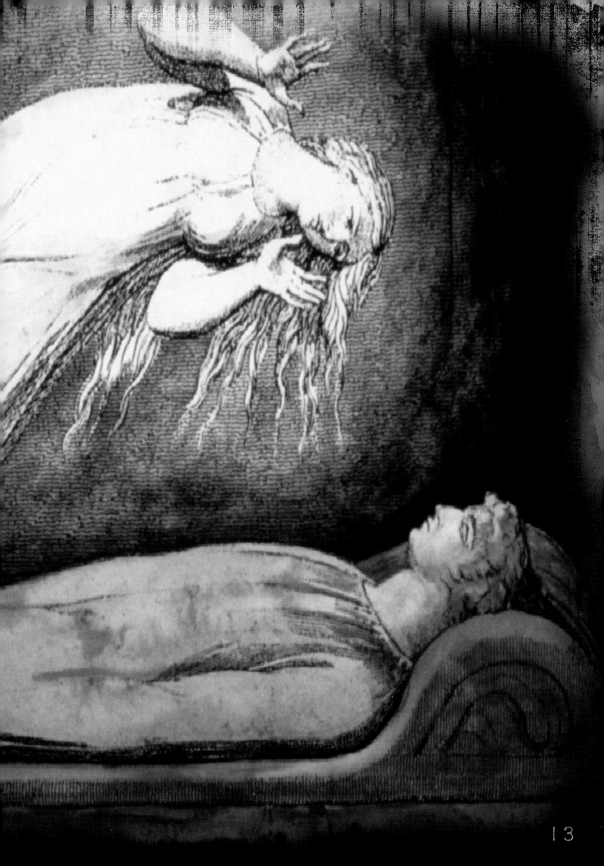

Many people say they went through a tunnel during their NDEs. They saw a bright light at the end of the tunnel.

NDE FACT

Most people who have had an NDE say the bright light made them feel loved.

FAMOUS EXPERIENCES

✳ Actress Jane Seymour had an NDE when she was sick with the flu. She left her body and saw herself on the bed. Seymour remembers begging the doctors to save her.

✳ Actor Eric Estrada had an NDE after a motorcycle accident. He went through a long hallway with bright lights. Then he heard a voice say, "You've got to go back."

✳ Actress Elizabeth Taylor had an NDE in the late 1950s. The movie star died for five minutes during surgery. Taylor said she went through a tunnel toward a bright white light.

✳ Actor William Petersen had an NDE after he severely cut his finger. Petersen remembers going through a long tunnel with bright lights. Then he heard a voice say, "It's not your time."

STUDYING NDEs

NDE **researchers** study these experiences. They have found that most people report similar NDEs.

researcher — someone who studies to find out about a subject and to learn new information

NDE
FACT

Children have NDEs
that are much like those
reported by adults.

Many people say they could see what happened around them during their NDEs. These people are usually right about what they saw.

NDE FACT

People who have been blind their whole lives say they could see during their NDEs.

Researchers say that people change after an NDE. Most people are no longer afraid to die.

NDE FACT

NDEs often include seeing a family member who has already died.

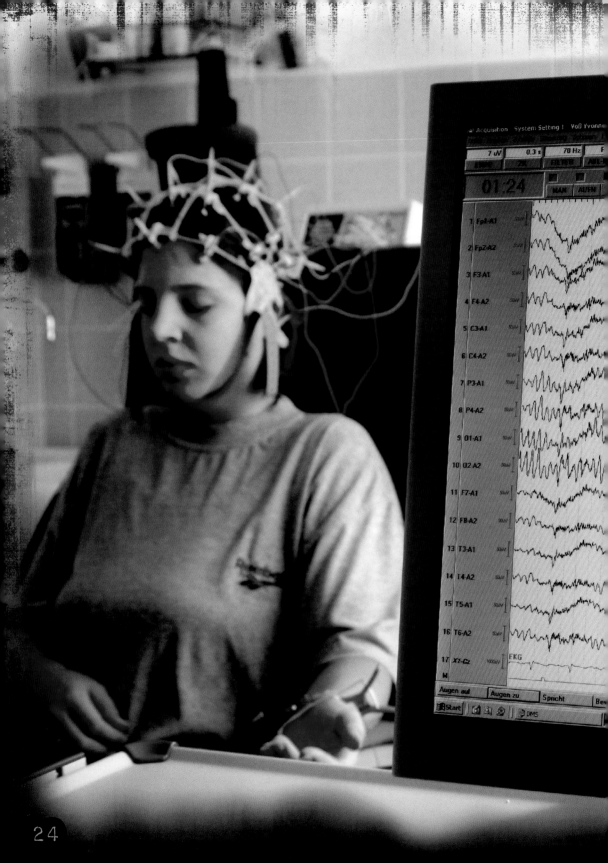

FACT OR FICTION?

Some scientists think NDEs are just dreams. The dreams happen when a person's brain does not get enough **oxygen**.

oxygen — a colorless gas in the air that people breathe

NDE researchers disagree. They say a lack of oxygen causes different types of **visions**.

NDE FACT

NDE researchers say visions caused by a lack of oxygen are not as emotional as NDEs.

vision — something seen, as in a dream

27

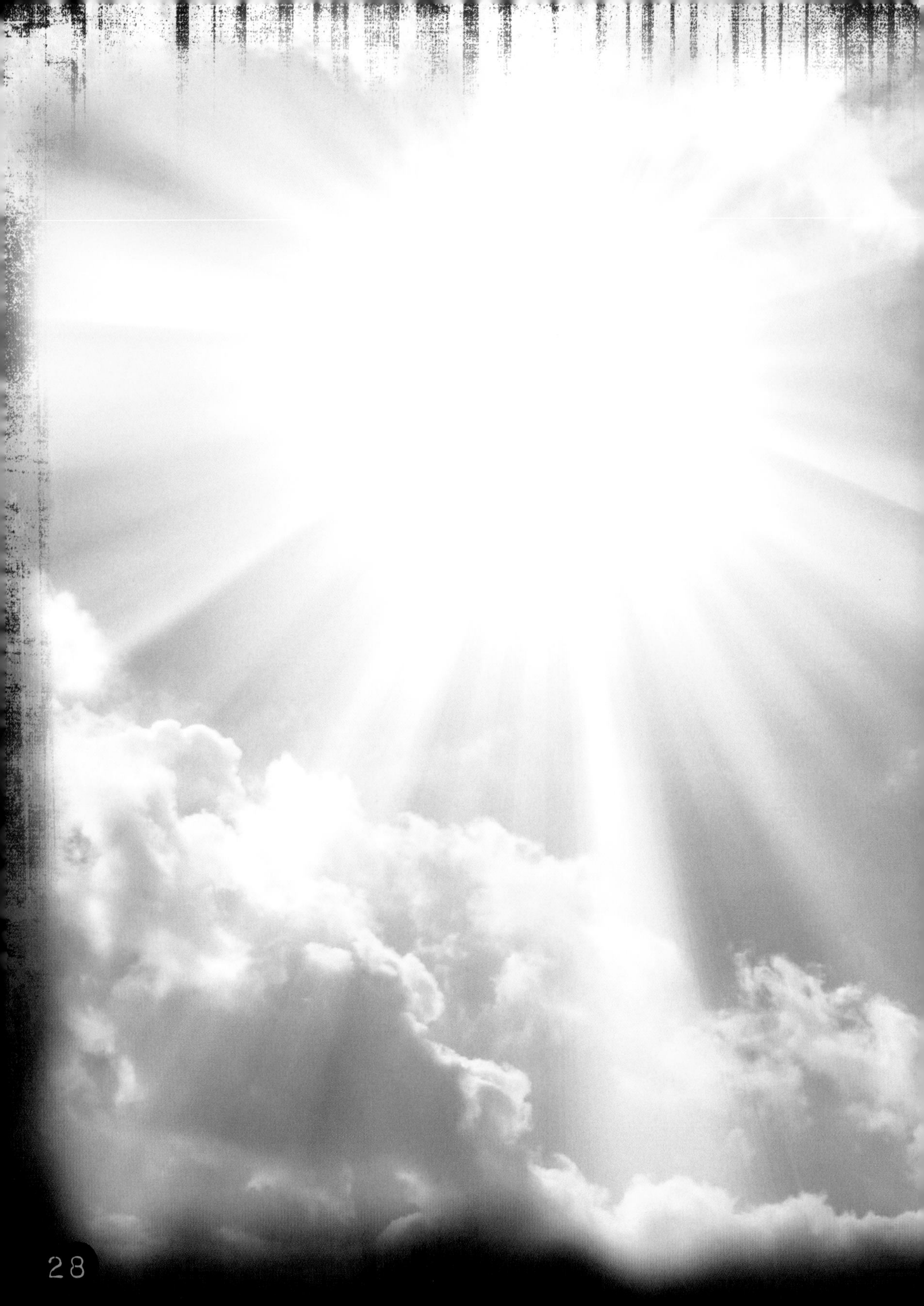

What do you think? Are NDEs real? Maybe someday we will know the answers.

GLOSSARY

emotional (i-MOH-shuh-nuhl) — having or causing strong feelings

morgue (MORG) — a place where dead bodies are kept at a hospital

oxygen (OK-suh-juhn) — a colorless gas that people breathe; humans and animals need oxygen to live.

pulse (PUHLSS) — a steady beat or throb felt as the heart moves blood through the body

researcher (REE-surch-ur) — someone who studies to find out about a subject and to learn new facts

revive (ri-VIVE) — to bring someone back to life

vision (VIZH-uhn) — something seen, as in a dream

READ MORE

Allen, Judy. *Unexplained: An Encyclopedia of Curious Phenomena, Strange Superstitions, and Ancient Mysteries.* Boston: Kingfisher, 2006.

Lynette, Rachel. *The Afterlife.* Mysterious Encounters. Farmington Hills, Mich.: Kidhaven Press, 2008.

Martin, Michael. *Near-Death Experiences.* The Unexplained. Mankato, Minn.: Capstone Press, 2005.

INTERNET SITES

FactHound offers a safe, fun way to find educator-approved Internet sites related to this book.

Here's what you do:

1. Visit *www.facthound.com*
2. Choose your grade level.
3. Begin your search.

This book's ID number is 9781429623292.

FactHound will fetch the best sites for you!

INDEX